LIFE INSURANCE

Published by Self Publish -N- 30 Days

Printed in the United States of America
ISBN: 978-1973949855

1. Self Defense 2. Success-Psychological Aspects
LB Personal Training: Life Insurance

Disclaimer/Warning:

LIFE INSURANCE

Basic Guide for Women's Safety and Self Defense

LeCarlo Beaty

www.selfpublishn30days.com

Book *LeCarlo Beaty* Today
443-402-6093 local
info@lecarlobeaty.com
www.lecarlobeaty.com

IG:lecarlo_beaty
FB:lecarlobeatycoaching

Private and Group Classes
Corporate Wellness
High Schools
Colleges
Women Self Defense Parties
Kids & Teens

I started Rising Strength with the goal of offering free self-defense classes and to raise awareness to the violence that occurs against women. I have spoken at and organized self-defense classes at high schools, colleges and businesses across the country. In February of 2016, I met LeCarlo Beaty after sharing the story of my attack at a self-defense class that he was teaching. I was so impressed with LeCarlo's class and how much fun that the women were having while also learning life-saving skills. The reasons behind why women choose to take a self-defense class can often evoke fear and anxiety but in LeCarlo's classes women are immediately at ease and know that they are in a relaxed and safe environment.

After taking LeCarlo's class, I started contacting LeCarlo to teach all of the self-defense classes that I organize. We have brought self-defense classes to women of all ages and have not had a class yet that wasn't both powerful and fun. Organizing free self-defense class-

es, sharing my story and connecting with other victims of violence has been cathartic and has help turned my story into something that helps others. Without taking self-defense classes so soon after the attack I'm not sure where I would be today.

Thanks,

Rachel

CONTENTS

INTRODUCTION

I have been working out most of my life. I can remember getting my first weight set in middle school. The old concrete filled kind. I also love to play sports. My dad played sports growing up and continued until a few years ago, but he is still in the gym. We workout together to the day when I'm home visiting. I played baseball (my favorite), football (only because I wanted to hit someone), ran track some, and even a little basketball. This was all up through high school. Once in college (Virginia State University), I tried out for football and even went to a few baseball meetings, but all I could think about was how tough it would be to do both sports and academics. Virginia State University was smaller back then. Going to school for an engineering degree was challenging. Most of my core engineering classes tended to be around the time for practice. All I knew was I wanted to be an engineer and my folks said, "don't mess up our money." So school it was. Not giving up being active I frequented the gym on campus.

Fast forward a few years, and I was working in Maryland playing softball for my company. One day I got hurt and went to the doctor to get checked out. I weighed in at 260 pounds; I was shocked. But the crazy thing was when she told me that I instantly was in agreeance. I felt terrible; big, slow and achy. At that point, I made a decision to get my health on track and started taking fitness seriously. I was working out, but I had the mindset that if I'm going to the gym, I can eat what I want......I was wrong. So that set in years of learning and working toward new health goals.

I was in a new gym in the area we currently live and just felt like I had enough of just lifting heavy things and putting them down. So I ended my membership and began to look for something else to help promote a healthy lifestyle. After some time I came across and interest in trying out Brazilian jiu-jitsu (BJJ) and Mixed martial arts (MMA). This turned out to be great. Something I know that I can do forever and stay in fantastic shape. Now training for a decade, I came to realize that I know a thing or two about dropping weight (maintaining 185 for the last six years or so) and how to defend myself.

2014 was the year that I became a certified personal trainer. Most people knew that I trained in BJJ/MMA as well and would ask about learning something to defend themselves. What I notice that when at the academy There were very few women that came in. When they did, they didn't last long. There was always a handful from when I began but nothing to scream about. So at this time, I decided to teach women self-defense classes. I know that coming into a gym and being a ton of males can be intimidating especially if you learn that you have to get up close and personal with complete strangers. Being in a female only environment and being able to speak about the issues women think about helps the process of learning self-defense.

What motivated me, even more, is that we had a beautiful baby girl and I thought about her future and wanted to make sure that she knew how to protect herself from an early age. So much so that its muscle memory before the age of independence comes. I want to be the parents that don't have to worry about our daughter but about the unlucky boy that decides to try something baby girl doesn't like. Insert evil grin. But while thinking about this, I think of all the things that happen to women, but learning self-defense never seems to be on the radar. They will stand by mace, knives, guns, etc. to protect themselves but never a lesson on defending themselves. Weapons, in my opinion, are a crutch and provides a false sense of security. Statistically speaking most violent attack come from people that you know or are familiar with. So having these weapons may do you more harm that good. Beside the fact of who commits these crimes, you have to get to the weapon to use it. If all you have ever done for self-defense is go to target practice, what do you do when you come out a store, and someone is right up on you? Go for your gun and show the perpetrator there is something worth having in your purse? Or fumble around with mace hoping not to miss or worse, use it on yourself.

This is why learning self-defense is a great thing. It helps you to get away to safety and perhaps your weapon. I have been holding classes for a few years and talking to women in the classes and truth be told never thought about a book. I changed my circle of influence and just talking to them and thinking differently they showed me that I have something that I can share with others. This book by no means is a very technical read. I wanted to create something that is practical and easy to understand. I wanted something that would help get your mind working in the right direction and start to think personal safety. People have auto insurance, home insurance, medical insurance to protect those things that are important. However, no one thinks about self-defense, something that can keep you safe. Self-defense is real Life Insurance. Why not protect what's important, your family and yourself.

Violence against women is a real problem all around the world I don't want to get into too much here because I mention statistics in a later chapter. Most violence is perpetrated by someone known to the victim. Stranger danger is still a real problem as well, but statistically speaking women experience violence from someone they know at a much higher rate. Women that are in the age range from 16 to 24 are at the greatest risk of experiencing violence. This makes sense if you think about it. This is the age range where individuals start to become independent and doing for themselves maybe even moving out on their own. But also this is where relationships start picking up which means that they are dating men that are about the same age. The old saying that hurt people hurt people can start to show here. If you grew up in an abusive environment, you are more likely to perpetrate the same behavior. So if a boy grows up seeing his dad abuse his mom then when he gets in a relationship he may do the same thing as that is his only example of a relationship. This can be for both the man or woman.

I want to help women become empowered and educated through personal safety and self-defense training so that they can face the world with more confidence.

CHAPTER 1

ABOUT ATTACKS

ABOUT ATTACKS

For a crime to take place, there have to be three things in place. Desire, Ability, and Opportunity. This is known as the triangle of crime. If one of these items are denied, then that in and of itself, can prevent a crime from happening. As it is with most things, this is only true if you are paying attention to your surroundings.

Most perpetrators of violent crime want it to be as easy as possible. In their minds they have a plan of action they are going to follow and a fighting his target is not usually part of that plan. If there is a chance of the target putting up a fight and making their plan risky or difficult they will many time pass on that target and find another that seems to be an ideal victim.

The truth is that most confrontations can be prevented or avoided altogether by most people.

Situational awareness will help in the area of preventing and avoiding dangerous situations. Many people that have been a victim of various types of attacks have stated things like "they took me by surprise" or "he came out of nowhere." If these people were paying attention, it is highly unlikely that would have been "taken by surprise." Even if these people were surprised, with training, they could have better defended themselves against the attack.

Let's take a moment to mention more conventional attacks. Here are results research completed but the National Institute of Justice. Sexual violence may occur in any relationship, but most perpetrators of sexual assault are known to their victims. Women are more likely to be victims of sexual abuse than are men. Women are significantly more likely than men to be injured during an assault. Sexual violence may begin early in life (under the age of 18) and in some cases early abuse can equal later victimization. Assault among college women. Sexual assault in intimate partner relationships (40-50% of battered women).

(https://www.nij.gov/topics/crime/rape-sexual-violence/Pages/victims-perpetrators.aspx)

Martial arts schools are a great place to learn techniques to defend oneself, build confidence and get physical exercises. The reality is that assaults and violence against victims are unpredictable, chaotic, fast and violent. Because of this typically one style of martial arts may lack in areas that are needed for a target to defend themselves. You should learn something that has a great variety of techniques such as standing, grappling, and fighting defending from the ground. By learning various positioning, you will start to build a toolset that will help you defend from a variety of possible attacks. Even though attacks can be dynamic by having a set of tools at your disposal in the techniques that you learn, you can better assess a situation and help to defend yourself because you know how to do something.

In any attack, the attacker will have a perceived advantage over you. After all, that is why they chose you as a victim in the first place. An attacker doesn't think, "I'm going to approach that lady, she is going to briefly pause and then scream, fight and run from me, while I attempt to take her purse."......They are thinking in a matter of factly way; this is going to happen like "A, B, C" then I'm going away with no problems. It is up to the target to be aware enough to deny the perpetrator one of the sides of the crime triangle. But if you are easily distracted and find it hard to stay aware then you need to learn self-defense so that you have a fighting chance to get away.

When it comes to self-defense, there is one and only one goal, and that is to get away to safety. This may take different forms. Such as having to make sure to incapacitate your attacker to make sure that you can get away. Or it could be a stun and run situation, or maybe evading/running from your attacker. If you are with someone that may not be able to defend themselves like an elderly family member or a child, you may need to stand your ground and fight while that person can get away to safety. The best way to prevent injury and to come to face an attack is to avoid a confrontation from happening in the first place.

There are many types of attacks that can take place. There are assault and battery incidents, domestic violence, dating violence, workplace/school bullying, and even sexual assaults. But with all of them denying one side of that crime triangle can help prevent an assault or attack. Awareness place a huge role in this. Being aware of your surroundings and also being self-aware to see if you are putting yourself in dangerous situations.

For me, I like to think of self-defense as real life insurance. Everyone has some insurance – auto, health, business, home, life, death, etc. The reason for all of these are the same; you need them in case something bad happens. It could be years before you are in a car accident, but you still have and pay for car insurance. But I always wonder why not self-defense? I don't plan to have to defend myself, but if the need arises, I want to be prepared. In the case of self-defense, I believe It is better to have and not need than to need and not have.

EMOTIONAL SIDE OF ATTACKS

If there is one thing that should help people learn to defend themselves it is so that they do not have to deal with the emotional side of attacks. Violent attacks can have psychological, emotional, and physical effects on a survivor. These can be violent in nature or sexual. Some of the effects can be Self-Harm, Depression, Anxiety, Sexually Transmitted Infections, Low Self Confidence, Low Self Esteem, Substance Abuse, Dissociation, Eating

Disorders, Pregnancy, Sleep Disorders, Flash-backs, PTSD, and Suicide. (https://www.rainn.org/effects-sexual-violence) These effects are not always easy to deal with but people should do their best to receive help and others should do their best to recognize when someone may be in need of help and take appropriate steps to help facilitate recovery.

FINAL THOUGHT ON ATTACKS

There is a saying that hurt people hurt people. Yes, there are many individuals who seem to be born with bad intentions. On the other side of the coin is that many times a victim can turn into an abuser. Someone who is sexually abused at a young age may grow up and in a few years victimize someone themselves. Also if someone is in violent domestic situations and are young, the may also become perpetrators of domestic violence because that's all they know.

It is important for people to learn to protect themselves and also pass that knowledge on to the younger generation. Knowing the effects of being a victim should be enough to want to stop them before it happens. Self-defense and self-protection are very important, but many

Notes

_____

_____

_____

_____

_____

_____

_____

_____

_____

_____

_____

_____

CHAPTER 2

WHY WOMEN NEED SELF-DEFENSE

WHY DO WOMEN NEED TO TAKE SELF-DEFENSE?

First off I would like to say that the most important reason that a woman or man for that matter should learn self-defense because you're are
worth being safe and protected. No one is going
to always be around to protect you from danger like a parent may keep a child from getting
hurt while playing. Once you get older, you will
start to explore and do things on your own, and
your parents or family will not always be around
to protect you when something happens. You
should value yourself enough to know that you
are something special and know that you can depend on yourself if the time comes and you have
switched from victim to victor. Your number one
job is to get back home or to your loved ones.

There are many reasons why women do not train for self-defense. Some of these reasons or excuses seem like real obstacles. But with anything in life, it has to be a priority. Going to work for people is a priority, even if they do not like their job, they know that they have to provide for their families and themselves. People say that eating healthy is too expensive but eat out 2 or 3 times a week, when that money can go to buy healthier foods. People say that they don't have time to workout, but you can see them waste hours away talking on the phone, on social media, and watching tv. The same can be said about the self-defense. It cost to much, or they don't have time. But the reality is both are all about priority. If a class in $50, for example, someone will say it costs too much. But those same people may go out that same day and spend $100 on clothes and shoes that they don't need.

There are a couple of other reason that I think hit home more and are at the root of the excuses. The first being intimidation. Most self-defense classes are run by men and can seem intimidating. Take a look at most martial arts studios especially MMA/BJJ academies. It's mostly men, and they are punching each other slamming one another on the mats and wrestling and grabbing each other all over. That can be very intimidating to a woman that may want to start training. The second is fear. If you think about what the training is for, you have to face the fact that bad things can happen and it may happen to you. Just like death and the reason why so many people pass away with no life insurance and leave their families in a financial crisis. When you sign up for a self-defense class, you are acknowledging that you could be attacked or that someone with you may be in danger of attack and may have to step in. But with all the statistics about an attack and the fact that women are targeted more for certain types of crime you would think that more women would take training or more organizations would provide training for females.

As I stated before, a self-defense class is real life insurance. No one has a problem paying $300/mo for car insurance for 15 years or cell phone insurance for their iPhone or Android. The crazy thing is that many people don't have death insurance and there are only a handful of guarantees in life, and one is that you are going to die. With all the science that shows eating healthy and exercising can extend your life and give you a better quality of life when you age, many people still do not do those things either. I consider health and fitness life insurance as well. However, when it comes to protecting yourself, many people hope something doesn't happen, believe that someone else will save them, or in some cases have a false sense of security because of some weapon. The issue with the weapons is that you have to get to it before it can do you any good and also there is the greater chance that it will be used against you.

Women have been attacked all kinds of ways just like men. However, women are targeted more for sexual assault crimes and are victims more in domestic violence incidents and stalking situations.

What is sexual assault? The term sexual assault refers to sexual contact or behavior that occurs without the explicit consent of the victim. Some forms of sexual assault include:

- Attempted rape

- Fondling or unwanted sexual touching

- Forcing a victim to perform sexual acts, such as oral sex or penetrating the perpetrator's body

- Penetration of the victim's body, also known as rape

(https://www.rainn.org/articles/sexual-assault)

It's unfortunate, but there is a rape culture that is prevalent everywhere we seem to look. There are instances that frequently occur on college campuses, places of work, and even just out on the streets. It appears that this is tolerated, expected and even the norm is some cases. For years it seems that the cause or reason for rape was always placed on the victims. What was she wearing, where was she, what time was it, etc.? Never was the blame placed on the attacker. There are two choices here: do women wait for men to be taught that NO means NO? Or should women take the proactive route and learn to protect themselves from men? I say the second choice.

As a whole, women continue to deny the need for their self-protection. Some of this is that fact that many relying instead on the law or someone else protecting them. In reaching out to women to offer self-defense training, I remember plenty of statements such as, "I'm okay, I grew up with brothers," "I'm crazy, don't no one want to mess with me," or "I carry so I'm good in that area." Statistically speaking the reality is that the ones women expect to protect them are the majority of the attackers committing the violent assaults. But the reality is there is also the chance of the stranger attack taking place as well. Look at the news and social media there are plenty of examples of attacks and violence against women. There are reports of joggers being sexually assaulted, assaults on campuses, celebrities attacking their significant others, and to all the cases of missing women. It is better to prepare to face the reality of an attack before you are confronted with the fear that comes with being attacked.

Women between the ages of 18-24 are at the greatest risk of assaults. This is the age range where many young people are going out on their own, starting relationships, and perhaps living on their own for the first time. Most people, especially women, do not take any self-defense or awareness training in preparation for this time. Also in this age range kids are getting into some of their first relationships. This could be where red flags may start to show in relationships, but if you don't know what to look for then, the relationship can take a wrong turn.

Men and women are both attacked. But there are different dynamics when it comes to a man or women being targeted. With a man, the assailant wants the victim's things or his life. But for a woman, there is the third, her body. Many women like to please everyone, don't want to seem like the are rude or want to be helpful, and this can put them in dangerous situations. Predators know this, so helping the injured guy on the stoop by helping put groceries in the house could have an awful ending for them. So it is important that women learn that it's ok to say no and have boundaries in place to keep them safe.

So why should women take self-defense?

- Violence can happen to anyone at anytime.

- Builds confidence

- Increases awareness

- Be a role model to other young ladies

- It is real life insurance

- Do it for the people that depend on you

- Peace of mind

The following are statistics from various sources that show the assaults and violence that exist towards women. My goal is to help women to realize the reality of this violence. The truth is much life insurance; people don't want to face the wrong that exists in the world.

STATS

Every 98 seconds, an American is sexually assaulted.

And every 8 minutes, that victim is a child. Meanwhile, only 6 out of every 1,000 perpetrators will end up in prison.

Perpetrators of Sexual Violence Often Know the Victim

The majority of children and teen victims know the perpetrator.

Of sexual abuse cases reported to law enforcement, 93% of juvenile victims knew the perpetrator.

- 59% were acquaintances
- 34% were family members
- 7% were strangers to the victim

ABOUT PERPETRATORS

Stats on dating violence

From www.loveisrespect.org

Young adult dating violence is a significant problem, affecting youth in every community across the nation. Learn the facts below.

TOO COMMON

Nearly 1.5 million high school students nationwide experience physical abuse from a dating partner in a single year.

One in three adolescents in the U.S. is a victim of physical, sexual, emotional or verbal abuse from a dating partner, a figure that far exceeds rates of other types of youth violence.

One in 10 high school students has been purposefully hit, slapped or physically hurt by a boyfriend or girlfriend.

WHY FOCUS ON YOUNG PEOPLE?

Girls and young women between the ages of 16 and 24 experience the highest rate of intimate partner violence — almost triple the national average.

Among female victims of intimate partner violence, 94% of those age 16-19 and 70% of those age 20-24 were victimized by a current or former boyfriend or girlfriend.

Violent behavior typically begins between the ages of 12 and 18.

The severity of intimate partner violence is often greater in cases where the pattern of abuse was established in adolescence.

DON'T FORGET ABOUT COLLEGE STUDENTS

Nearly half (43%) of dating college women report experiencing violent and abusive dating behaviors.

College students are not equipped to deal with dating abuse – 57% say it is difficult to identify and 58% say they don't know how to help someone who's experiencing it.

One in three (36%) dating college students have given a dating partner their computer, online access, email or social network passwords and these students are more likely to experience digital dating abuse.

One in six (16%) college women have been sexually abused in a dating relationship

From www.ncadv.org

NATIONAL STATISTICS

On average, nearly 20 people per minute are physically abused by an intimate partner in the United States. During one year, this equates to more than 10 million women and men.

1 in 3 women have been victims of [some form of]

physical violence by an intimate partner within their lifetime.

1 in 4 women have been victims of severe physical violence by an intimate partner in their lifetime.

1 in 7 women have been stalked by an intimate partner during their lifetime to the point in which they felt very fearful or believed that they or someone close to them would be harmed or killed.

Intimate partner violence accounts for 15% of all violent crime.

Women between the ages of 18-24 are most commonly abused by an intimate partner.

Domestic victimization is correlated with a higher rate of depression and suicidal behavior.

RAPE

1 in 5 women and 1 in 71 men in the United States has been raped in their lifetime.

Almost half of female (46.7%) and male (44.9%) victims of rape in the United States were raped by an acquaintance. Of these, 45.4% of female rape victims and 29% of male rape victims were raped by an intimate partner.

STALKING

19.3 million women and 5.1 million men in the United States have been stalked in their lifetime.1 60.8% of female stalking victims and 43.5% men reported being stalked by a current or former intimate partner.

BULLYING

Let's not forget about bullying. (www.dosome-thing.org)

Over 3.2 million students are victims of bullying each year.

Approximately 160,000 teens skip school every day because of bullying.

17% of American students report being bullied 2 to 3 times a month or more within a school semester. Take a stand in your community by hosting a Bullying Policy Makeover event customizing your school's anti-bullying policy.

1 in 4 teachers see nothing wrong with bullying and will only intervene 4% of the time.

By age 14 less than 30% of boys and 40% of girls will talk to their peers about bullying.

Over **67%** of students believe that schools respond poorly to bullying, with a high percentage of students believing that adult help is infrequent and ineffective.

71% of students report incidents of bullying as a problem at their school.

90% of 4th through 8th graders report being victims of bullying.

1 in 10 students drops out of school because of repeated bullying.

As boys age, they are less and less likely to feel sympathy for victims of bullying. In fact, they are more liable to add to the problem than solve it.

Physical bullying increases in elementary school, peaks in middle school and declines in high school. Verbal abuse, on the other hand, remains constant.

Looking at a few of the stats:

- 1 in 3 – Women murdered by intimate partner
- 1 in 4 – College women victims of attempted or completed sexual assault

- 1 in 6 – Will be victim of attack

- 1 in 7 – Women have been stalked

- 1 in 5 – teens experience dating sexual/physical violence

- 1 in 3 – teens report abuse

- 1 in 4 – Have been cyberbullied more than once

age 16-24 – more vulnerable to intimate partner violence

Just these few statistics show that violence is prevalent everywhere. Don't get me wrong, men are victimized as well, but women are targeted at a higher rate than men. These numbers alone show the need for people, especially women to take it upon themselves to learn how to prevent and defend themselves from these type of incidents. Just like your car, house, and phone you need insurance in case something happens to you. Learning skills to help build awareness, prevent, avoid dangerous situations and as a last resort defend yourself is something that everyone needs. How much is your life worth to you? Your spouse? Your kids? Your family? Your friends?

Notes

Notes

Notes

Notes

CHAPTER 3

WHAT PREDATORS LOOK FOR

What I have found since training is that the more I learn to fight the less I want to. If there is a situation, I try to think of a way to get away from it and use physical tactics as a last resort. It seems that the same stands true for others. The more you are prepared to handle a violent situation, the less likely you are to find yourself in those situations. If someone has been a victim to these before or worried about them, these incidents stop or don't happen at all. Once you learn self-defense, the benefits are significant and show through your body language, awareness, and fitness levels. People who train in self-defense are better prepared to handle situations of harassment or bullying.

HOW ARE VICTIMS CHOSEN

Psychologists have known for many years that predators chose their victims based off of signals given off by the victim. Much in the same way predators in the wild choose prey. Lions will go after a lame or isolated gazelle. These signal can be known or unconscious to the victim.

THE GRAYSON/STEIN STUDY

Researchers, Betty Grayson and Morris I. Stein, In 1984 two conducted a study to determine what criteria predators use to select their victims. Part of the process was that they videotaped several pedestrians on a busy New York City sidewalk without their knowledge. Afterward, they later showed the tape convicts that were in prison for violent crimes such as rape, murder, robbery, etc. Then the psychologist informed the criminals to identify which people in the video would make a perfect victim. What they found were interesting.

Within only a few seconds participants made their choices. What was astonishing to the researchers was almost all the convicts chose the same people as victims. Those that many would think would be selected as a victim were passed and vice versa. The selection was not dependent on race, age, size or gender.

The convicts at the time didn't even understand why they chose who they chose. From this experiment, it became apparent that predator wanted their victim unconsciously. And that victims gave off signals that they would be easy targets.

The researchers realized the criminals were assessing the ease with which they could overpower the objectives based on several nonverbal signals:

Posture: A slumped posture is indicative of weakness or submissiveness. A downward gaze implies preoccupation and being unaware of one's surroundings. Also, someone reluctant to establish eye contact can be perceived as submissive. These traits indicate an ideal target for a predator.

Body language: Victims lacked "wholeness" in their body movement. They swung their arms as if they were detached and independent from the rest of their body. Non-victims moved their body from their "center" as a coordinated whole implying strength, balance, and confidence.

Pace of walking: Victims tend to walk at a different rate than non-victims. Usually, they walk slower than the flow of pedestrian traffic. Their movement lacks a sense of deliberateness or purpose. However, an unnaturally rapid pace can project nervousness or fear.

Length of stride: People selected as victims had an exaggerated stride: either abnormally short or long. They dragged, shuffled or lifted their feet unnaturally as they walked. Non-victims, on the other hand, tended to have a smooth, natural gate. They stepped in a heel-to-toe fashion.

Awareness of environment: Distraction is another cue criminals look for. Some people think talking on a cell phone enhances their safety because the other person can always summon help if there's trouble—but experts disagree.

Neither criminals nor victims were consciously aware of these cues. They are what psychologists call "precipitators," personal attributes that increase a person's likelihood of being criminally victimized.

(https://www.psychologytoday.com/articles/200901/marked-mayhem)

(http://www.protectivestrategies.com/victim-se-lection.html)

And when it comes to rapists these same team found that rapist was more capable than most people to interpret facial cues, such as a downward gaze or a fearful expression that allowed them to spot passive, submissive women.

Other things that attributed to being selected as a victim were drugs and alcohol, environment, being flashy.

OTHER AREAS THAT AFFECT SELECTION

If you remember the crime triangle, there need to be three things present. Desire - which we know the perpetrator has, ability and opportunity. Other criteria can be used to select a victim as well the works in conjunction with opportunity.

Location. The attacker looks for places that can trap the victim so that there is little chance of escape. This could be to murder or rape them. The location can isolate the victim given them little chance to survive as well, but also a better opportunity for the attacker to get away. Locations like parking garages, alleys, stairwells, trails, etc. Also, these kind of areas helps with the element of surprise which helps them because if you don't know its coming, it can cause you to become flooded with fight or flight responses and even to freeze which will assist the perpetrator to complete their attack. How about these other locations? How could someone best attack you in these places?

- Your residence

- While walking or running

- While driving in public

- At school or workplace

- Shopping locations

- Sporting and any recreational venue

- Restaurants

Even though most predators want an easy target. There are cases of those that want their victim to fight back. This is something that you should keep in mind. Most attackers want an easy target. It has been proven that if you fight back, you have a great chance to escape serious harm.

PREDATORS AND TACTICS

Gavin de Becker (The Gift of Fear) covers seven tactics a predator commonly uses to gain your trust or take advantage of you:

Forced Teaming: Using the word "we" to establish a relationship or show you have something in common.

Charm: Charm requires an effort. If a stranger is charming, He wants something from you. Charm is an action, not a personality trait.

Too Many Details: Too many details to make his story more believable.

Typecasting: A predator will often attempt to put you in a group you don't want to be in, so you'll do extra trying to prove you're not what he says you are. Maybe he says he thought you were cool but your just like all the other annoying girls, just to have sex with you, even though you may not want to

Loan Sharking: The predator does you a favor, which he hopes make you feel the need to reciprocate.

Unsolicited Promise: "I won't hurt you, I promise.", "I'm not crazy, I promise." If he's saying it, he's thinking about doing it.

Discounting the Word "No": When you tell them no, they'll disregard it try to get what they want from you.

If sit and think about these seven tactics I'm sure you can think of someone that has used them before or even you have used them. The difference is that most people don't have any sinister intent behind them. Maybe the person using them on you wants your number or wants a date, but the tactics are the same. If you are paying attention and aware, you will notice these. Your gut will make you feel uncomfortable. You must remember here to trust your instincts. If you feel scared it is a good thing, that is nature saying get out of there get away. If some stranger comes to you and is getting more personable that you think is typical, pay attention to your surroundings. The person you are speaking to may be up to something or have an accomplice nearby waiting to assist in a criminal act against you.

Notes

Notes

_____

_____

_____

_____

_____

_____

_____

_____

_____

_____

_____

_____

Notes

Notes

_____

_____

_____

_____

_____

_____

_____

_____

_____

_____

_____

_____

CHAPTER 4
BOUNDARIES AWARENESS

One of the first things to think about when preventing crime or violence is setting boundaries. Everyone has boundaries, and the key is to set them and stick to them. It is important to find your boundaries and use your voice to let others know what they are. The catch is to stand firm on your boundaries. If you're on a date and the guy decides to go further than you would, and you tell them no, it's ok. If you don't want to go further, that is up to you not them. It is your body, and you are the only one that is in control of it. If that person doesn't listen and decides to keep going, then you know that they don't have your best interest in mind. They are only out for what they want. The same thing can go for preventing possible attacks.

The previous example was for someone known to you. Now let's mention about someone that you don't know. For me when I'm in public I automatically start to pay attention to people that are about 5ft away. I'm not paranoid, but I will pay attention to see if they move closer or start looking "unnatural." I feel that this is important because if they are 5 ft away even if they tried to catch me off guard to surprise me, they would have to take at least two full strides to get to me. This is important because that will buy me time to react. If this person is within arm's length and decides to attack me, it will take little to no effort to get a jump on me. I don't want that to happen. Now there are situations where people will be close. Maybe an elevator, concert, store, etc. This could be a little tricky and again getting in a position to observe the most details about the environment is key and also not being distracted. Try to pay attention to everyone and take a look at the body language that they are putting out.

You should take a moment and do a self-assessment. How close is too close? Depending on a situation how far are you willing to let something go? When will you tell them to stop? What is ok and what is not ok? These are just a few questions that you can ask yourself. These questions can apply to all areas of your life. Daily activities, school, work, family, friends, and relationships. But here we are talking self-defense and self-protection. If you are walking down the sidewalk how close is too close for a stranger to get before you feel uncomfortable? Or maybe you think I won't be distracted. Will you allow the person that seems to need help get too close? Maybe he asks for the time and takes two steps to get closer to you. Or seems interested in a possible date? Do you back off? Do you tell him to stop getting closer? Do you even notice?

Setting boundaries can cover many areas such as material, physical, mental, emotional, sexual, and even spiritual. Sometimes it's hard to set boundaries for people. Have you ever wondered why? Since teaching classes, I get many women that state that they do wont to hurt anyone's feelings or seem like they are rude. In some attacks that have happened, people mention that they had a bad feeling about a person or situation. If that is the case why didn't they listen to it?

Many individuals find it hard to set boundaries. Setting boundaries is a learned behavior. The best way to set boundaries is to take a look at all areas of your life that was mentioned earlier (material, physical, mental, emotional, sexual, daily activities, school, work, family, friends, and relationships.). In order to set these boundaries, you first have to know what is ok with you and what is not ok. Once you decide what is ok with you, let others know. I'm not saying write them down and pass them out, what I am saying is if someone is doing something that you don't like say something to them and mean it. For instance, if you are at a party and some guy has had one too many drinks. He decides to put his arm around you maybe he is trying to pick you up, or he could just have his arm around you while still screaming and yelling with his buddies. Either way, you don't want his arm around you. This is where you tell him, tell him again, and if he does not comply, you tell him one last time while removing his arm from your body. The next step is to practice, practice, practice. People in your life will always ask for something. If deep down you don't want to do it... don't. This is your life, body, or material things. You don't owe anyone anything.

Once you say no, stick to it, and you don't have to explain yourself. Don't worry about hurting people's feelings or being seen as rude or stuck up. Make sure to stick to your boundaries and use them all the time. Setting boundaries will also help with building confidence. Anyone that tries to discount your boundaries and make them seem unimportant doesn't have your best interests in mind. So that guy on the sidewalk who you told not to get closer starts moving in you already know what time it is. Or maybe you feel uncomfortable, and you ask the person that is 20 ft away "hey are you following me?" If they are not, more than likely, they will be a little embarrassed and assure you that they are not. But what if they are? Would you rather, find out when they are 20ft away rather than 5 ft away?

Your safety is the number one goal. If someone does not have bad intentions in mind, they will let it go with understanding. If they wanted more than they tried to lead you to believe, then their attitude and actions will also show you that you were correct in keeping your boundaries.

AWARENESS

Before any form of safety, self-defense, or preventive measures can be taken; one must be completely aware of yourself and your environments. The dynamics of personal safety are always changing. So one must be able to assess the environment for potential dangers at all times making adjustments as needed.

Many people know that one thing is true, you must trust your instincts, your gut feeling. Growing up my parents always told me if it doesn't look right, get away. But growing up you don't know what that means always. You have to have experiences to teach you what doesn't look right. Situation awareness starts with being able to observe your environment and what is going on. You have to set baselines of the environment. For example just because someone looks nervous doesn't mean they are ready to harm someone. What if you are at a train or bus station? This person could just be nervous about being on time to the next stop.

What is awareness or situational awareness? Situational awareness is your ability to identify, assess, and process information about your environment that will cause you to react in an appropriate manner. If something is dangerous, avoid it, if nothing is out of the ordinary, carry on as usual. The key to trusting your instincts is that you must be paying attention to all the things that are going on around you.

To increase your awareness, you must be in a position to gather as much information about your environment as possible. For instance, when I go to restaurants, I sit facing the door just in case this is the time that someone wants to come in and start attacking people I can see what is transpiring before my eyes and make appropriate adjustments to save my family, friends, myself and other people around me.

First of all, awareness is a choice. You must choose to be aware of your surroundings. Even with this, it is nearly impossible to think of all the possible scenarios that could take place. In this day and age, everyone is looking on their smartphones and has tunnel vision when talking to others. So to be aware of your environment is easy once you figure out what is distracting you. Get off the phone and look up and around. When you talk to others, scan your environment.

Always put yourself in a position to observe the most about your environment wherever you are.

You need to establish baselines so that you can determine what is and isn't a threat. Understand the differences between dominant and nondominant postures. What is normal or abnormal about an environment that you are in. For instance, someone wearing a trench coat in 80-degree weather would be out of place. There are six domains ("Left of Bang") that help to mold baseline for accessing your environment and threats:

- Kinesics: The study of body movement, which, upon being analyzed to uncover the meaning of the gesture, posture, or expression, becomes body language.

- Biometric Cues: The body's physiological responses to stress.

- Proxemics: Assessments made regarding interpersonal separation and body placement.

- Geographic: The relationship between people and their environment.

- Iconography: The visual representation of a person's (or group's) beliefs and affiliations.

- Atmospherics: The collective sense of safety in an area or situation.

The most important of the six domains is kinesics which has three areas of body language which are:

1.   Dominance/submissive

2.   Comfortable/uncomfortable

3.   Interested/uninterested

When you go out in the world take a look at people and compare them to the three areas of kinesics. For the most part, people are submissive, having a nondominant posture. People are comfortable, they don't look out of place, and most people are uninterested in what is going on around them. For example, you go to a park, and you see someone sitting on a bench, slouching deeply reading a book. This person more than likely is not a threat. Now if we flip that and we are at the bank on Friday waiting to cash a check and the person two people up is wearing a hat and glasses, postured up, looking back and forth and checking who enters the bank. We may get the sense that that person is about to be up to no good.

To review awareness is a choice. When you are aware you are observing what is happening in the environment, once you have established baselines it will be easier to orient yourself is what is taking place in the environment. After you observe and orient yourself, you have to decide to take action. This action could be nothing because there is not a threat or it could be for example leave because the three guys that walked in are about to cause trouble in the store that you are in.

The takeaway is that you must not be distracted and you must pay attention at all times. So many people are victims, and the first thing many of them say is that they were caught by surprise. I don't believe you can be caught by surprise if you are staying aware. If I'm walking and I'm about to walk through a doorway, I notice which side the wall will be on, move closer to that side and as I walk through glance to the other side to see if someone is there. If someone is there, they may be up close and personal, but because I looked first, I had that much more time to go from victim to victor.

HOW DO YOU GET BETTER AT AWARENESS?

Put yourself in the best position to observe as much of your environment as possible.

You can sharpen your skills by playing the awareness game. This would be for example: walking into a building, see if you can locate all the exists, places to hide, closest weapons in case things go south, how many people, how many workers, etc. Take a look at the three areas of body language above. Look at people and see if you can tell what is going on.

Working on building better awareness will help you to develop your baseline. This is important. For example crossed arms may show a person is uninterested, but what if the environment is inside and a bit chilly? Could this person just be cold? Maybe the guy in the corner looking nervous isn't about to do something bad, he could be anxiously waiting for someone to arrive. These are a couple of example of why building a baseline is important. Body language and body position can tell a lot about a situation. Being aware of this can help to avoid

Once you become more aware and can adequately assess your environment, learning to trust your gut or that funny feeling will be easy. It's hard to know what doesn't look right if you are never paying attention. Then you are "caught by surprise."

Notes

Notes

_____

_____

_____

_____

_____

_____

_____

_____

_____

_____

_____

_____

Notes

Notes

CHAPTER 5

PREVENTION

BAD TARGET

The first way to prevent an attack would be to be a bad target. As discussed early the signals that perpetrators are looking for are – Posture, body language, stride rate, balance, awareness, confidence. Again these signals are sometimes known, but mostly unknown. If you think about a person who is victimized multiple times by different people, why is that person targeted? The same goes for individuals who claim there are no good men/women because they all do XYZ. The right statement is what is it about me that is attracting those type of people.

The first thing that will no doubt help is paying attention to your environment. Kill the distractions!!! Put yourself in the position to observe the most you can about what is going on. Look for people in uncommon areas, that odd pairing of

2 people on the sidewalk looking around looking shifty. Next, take a look at your body language, are you giving off confidence or defeat? Are you walking with a purpose or like you are kind of unsure where you are going? Another thing to think about is what items do you have in hand. Are you walking in $100 heels, carrying a $500 bag, wearing diamonds and gold? Nothing wrong with this, but you are offering a low-risk high reward for the perpetrator. They could do a hit and run. Grab your purse and go. At the least, the purse is worth some cash, and if you are carrying that purse, it's a good chance something else of value is in there. The last thing I would like to mention is not being in places where things could likely happen such as the bar and clubs at 2:00 am. or drinking heavily at a party with people you don't know. Going into an area that you know nothing about. Maybe it's a high crime area, perhaps there are gangs, and you have the wrong colors. These are all things to think about in moving about daily.

PREVENTION AND AVOIDING

Egos have put people in harm's way more than anything. As stated before for a crime to take place there need to be three things in place. Desire, Ability, and Opportunity. If you think, "I'm not going to back down," that is the wrong thought. You have no clue as to what the other person is capable of doing. Loud talking, swelling up, getting is someone's face may intimidate some people, but there are others out there that don't care about any of that and can and will with no thought physically attack you and may even injure you all because of ego. Sometimes it's better just to walk away.

Prevention can be one of the easiest ways to avoid a possible attack. Look at bars and fights. If you are going out on the town do you go to the local bar known for having many fights or do you decide to go to a lounge that has live jazz playing? Which would decrease your chance of having to defend yourself? If you are in school, do you attend the party that you know a rival will also be in attendance? Are you going to take the chance of getting into an altercation just because you want to go out? What about walking at night? Do you take the dark path between two buildings because you know it's faster? Or do you take a long way around? Those in between places are great for attacks. People don't hang out there, so the predator has a better chance to attack you and escape. This isn't to say be paranoid and never leave the house, but your choices can put you in harm's way. Again, violence can happen to anyone at anytime. Your job is to avoid it if at all possible.

Another good tactic is to keep distance between you and the perpetrator. If you are walking down the street and notice someone following you, cross to the other side and see if they pass as well. This doesn't mean too much it could be a coincidence. But cross back to the other side, did they follow you again? If they did, use the distance to slide into a building before they see you or turn a corner and go another direction or evade and hide in plain sight.

EVASION

Evasion is another good way to prevent an attack from happening. The main thing here is that if you may be caught and are far away from safety the next best thing to do is to become hard to find. If you know that you have to walk a particular path or maybe someone is following you, but you cannot run to safety, what can you do? For starters, you could hide if the perpetrator has not seen where you are. Maybe there is a car to hide behind, a wall, a large tree. What if the offender has seen you and is closing in, what can you do? Maybe you can run behind that car, keep a tree between you and the perpetrator all the while screaming "my baby my baby he has my baby"........Why this? Because "Fire" and "Help" don't work anymore. But who is not going to see what is happening to a child?

The key to evasion is to hide in plain sight or keep something between you and the perpetrator that will be enough to keep them away from you. Distance is prevention. If they cannot get to you, they cannot harm you, unless they have some weapon that they can shoot or throw at you to hurt you. And once you put up this kind of fight is the perpetrator going to keep trying to get to you, or run off and search for an easier target?

VERBAL SELF DEFENSE

Now, what if you cannot get away or evade a perpetrator? What is the next step? Using our voices.

This can be done in a few ways. You can leave – Maybe you're at a party, and you are not feeling the guy hitting on you. You can dominate – Telling them to back off or leave you alone. You can comply – Give them material items they want.

If you are paying attention and someone comes up to you, and you are aware, and your instincts are telling you something is not right then you set your boundaries. Tell the person to stop and that you don't feel comfortable. If they don't comply, you already know what time it is. However, let's say you are surprised it's going to be hard to say stop back up get away. The reason being is that they see you as the perfect target, no witnesses, perfect time, etc. Now you have to use other verbal defense.

This is where you seem to submit. The key is to make them feel like they are in control. What you are trying to do is get their guard to come down so that you can surprise attack. Fake the fear tell them you don't want to get hurt, but don't beg. If you know that you can get away, fake comply so that you can get away. Let's say you are at a party or dating someone and they want to take it all the way and will not take no for an answer. Instead of fighting physically, do it mentally. Hey, I want to just like you, but could I have another drink or could we move to the bedroom to get more comfortable. Now you are "giving" him what he wants his guard will be down. Now is your chance to run away.

PHYSICAL COMPLIANCE

If for some chance you are taken by surprise compliance is a way to prevent an attack. Remember to listen and stay in the current moment. Many time the predator will tell you what they want. Your purse, wallet, keys, phone, etc. Give it to them you can always recover those things. However, don't just hand them over, throw them away to the side. If the end goal was your material item, then the predator should go after them. If not then you know that its time to do what you have to do to protect yourself. But never ever ever ever go anywhere with anyone or allow them to take someone who is with you, family/friend. If they threaten you here what do you think will happen when they take you somewhere else? This is where you tell them you're not going anywhere and they will have to kill/hurt you right here right now.

PHYSICAL FITNESS

If you can remember the things that predators look for when selecting a victim some of them had to do with physical attributes. Walking, shoulder, confidence, and posture. Physical fitness is one thing that I know can help with these all. As a personal trainer, self-defense trainer and a Brazilian Jiu Jitsu practitioner, I can say that this is true. When you look at where you started and where you are you feel good about things. Maybe you lost 20lbs, used to do only four pushups now it's 25, never been in a fight but with training know that you can wrestle someone off of you or defend against punches. All of these help with building confidence. If no one else knows you know that you can do all these things and more. This will show in the way you walk and carry yourself.

If a predator looks your way and gets the feeling that you are a fighter, there is a good chance that he will pass on you and move to another potential target. The other side of being fit is that you can put up a fight and you will have the stamina to run away. The one side effect of being fit is that you may lose weight and like what you see in the mirror. Just keep that in mind going forward.

HOME SECURITY

Attacks at home are also an area that can be prevented or the chance of reduced. The number one thing is to make sure all your doors and windows are locked to your home and your car. That alone can deter criminals because breaking into a home may put them at risk of being caught. Next, on the outer perimeter, you can place motion lights, video cameras (real or fake), and an alarm system. These layers of protection will help to keep a criminal away.

Don't open the doors for strangers. Hopefully, you have a storm door. Leave it locked so that if you open your door to speak to someone, they will have a harder time trying to get to you and allowing you to close the door on them and keep them out. If you look in the news, you can see the stories of perpetrators posing as service and utility men. Always ask for identification, and you can always call the company to see if they indeed send a service rep out to your location.

Dogs are also a good option as well. Dogs make

noise and depending on the breed can visibly be a deterrent to a criminal attempting to invade your space.

Notes

Notes

Notes

_____

_____

_____

_____

_____

_____

_____

_____

_____

_____

_____

_____

Notes

_____

_____

_____

_____

_____

_____

_____

_____

_____

_____

_____

_____

CHAPTER 6
SAFETY STRATEGIES

Now I'm going to talk some about safety strategies and tips. This is by no means a complete list. What I want to do is give you a starting point to having or creating a habit of personal safety much like people create a habit of healthy living. Again, this is real life insurance; we want to hope for the best, but be prepared for the worst. Think about your day to day life. If you were going to attack yourself, where would you do it? Why? Fix it!!!

DAILY

- Kill the distractions. Don't walk and text; try not to be on the phone with someone for extended periods of time. This will help with staying aware of the people and things that are close to you. If you are consumed by something like a phone call or texting you may never see the person that is standing 1 foot away from your side.

- A little trick that I use when walking in the mall or on the streets is to glance at windows to see if anyone is following me or close enough to where I feel I need to pay attention to them.

- When you leave a building always glance in every direction to make sure no one is outside waiting for their next target. They may be close, but noticing them first can get you prepared to defend yourself faster.

- Don't waste time. When you get in your car, lock the door start her up and go. There have been many occasions where people get in the car and fumble with the radio, look for something in their purse/car, or they are texting/talking on the phone, and they are victimized.

- It is mostly said to kids, but adults need to watch out for strangers as well. Keep your distance; set your boundaries.

- Something that I do is when at a red light I like to leave enough space to pull off if I need to. Just in case someone wants to try to jump in the car or attack me.

- Pay attention to the environment and the people in it. Your gut instinct may feel the vibe that something isn't right and that will let you know to get away.

- Ladies keep a small wallet with all the valuable items in your pocket, just have your car/house key in your pocket as well. If someone tries to take the purse, throw it and run away.

- Cell phones are a popular item these days, keep it put away but if they try to get it, give it to them without resisting. You can always buy new stuff.

- Watch out for odd things as well. Such as something on the back window of your car. It blocks your view, and you will want to get out a move it. How did it get there? Just pull off and drive a bit then stop where people are to remove it.

- When driving never go under a ¼ tank of gas. This way you can choose where you want to refuel.

- Try to avoid going to the ATM at night. If you do make sure its well lit or you are with someone.

- Keep track of your credit report.

HOME

- Layers of security- means have a fence, then motion lights, perhaps cameras (real or fake), lock the entrances to your home, alarm system, perhaps dogs – they make noise. By having these, it can significantly reduce your chance of being a victim

- Do you live alone – Get an old pair of boots/ shoes from a male friend or goodwill. Leave them on the porch or at the front door. Get a couple of jackets as well. Buy some sports magazines and video game controllers and leave them on the tables. IF someone comes to the house, they will see these things and may not take the chance of having to deal with another man.

- Adding on to the previous one. If someone knocks on the door start yelling "I got it!!" "I got it it....it's the door!" Now you have given the impression that someone else is home as well.

- Do you live in an apartment? When you leave, place a $20 bill somewhere as if maybe you dropped it. If it's gone leave NOW. Don't stop with the money. Maybe leave a chair in an awkward position that would cause anyone to move it to go by. This is another sign. The key here is to notice the details.

- Look around the property to see if things look out of place. Maybe the garbage can is two ft over to the left than usual, footsteps leading from the gate. The screen door isn't closed all the way. Etc

- Make a safe room in the house. Old phones can still call 911. Leave the phone and the charger in the room with some form of weapon.

- Keep something near the door that you could use to stop the door opening all the way, also something to use as a weapon. An umbrella could work as a weapon. You can jab it through the slightly opened door.

- Wasp spray. It shoots 10ft away and meant to hit hives. Have a few around the house, and you can aim for the eyes and keep a safe distance to get away.

- Clean from around your doorways. You don't want anything there that can trip you up if a struggle happens at the door.

CAMPUS LIFE

- Visit the campus at night to see if there are danger zones to avoid.

- Learn the layout of the campus in case you have to run from danger you can run to safety.

- Walk the campus with friends or security at night

- Not everyone is a student

- Don't get drunk with people you don't know or trust

- Never leave your drink alone and only drink what you pour. Predators will slip something in there in no time.

- NO means NO …... Set your boundaries

- Stay on the path....No shortcuts

- What out for areas that provide good cover for attacks or hiding

- Take a self-defense class

- Lock your dorm doors

- Birds of a feather flock together – at least that's what most people believe. If you have "friends" that are all about partying and hooking up, then those guys are naturally going to believe that you are with the program as well or you wouldn't be there.

- If anything happens, try to remember as much as you can, keep evidence and report it right away.

- Keep social media tightly secured. Know your "friends" and don't share too much

- Keep your information locked up and safe in your dorm room.

- If you see a stranger in the dorm, ask who they are and what they want or tell the RA.

- Let others know where you are going

TRAVEL/HOTEL

- When driving never go under a ¼ tank of gas. This way you can choose where you want to refuel.

- Keep cash in your car for emergencies

- Keep doors locked at all times

- Park in well-lit areas and with other people around

- Keep your luggage with you

- Don't stay on the first floor

- Ask for a room that is not joined to another via an interior door.

- Check the room upon each arrival – shower closet under bed windows

- Use the safe for essential items

- Identify all escape routes upon arrival

- Obtain a couple of hotel business cards and place one by the phone in case you need to give location

- Bring a rubber door stopper

- Use the locks on the door.

- Use the do not disturb sign leave the tv when you leave out.

- If traveling out of the country check to see if there are any travel warnings for your destination or any stops along the way.

OUTDOORS

- Don't be distracted

- Remove headphones when running or walking. You need to be able to hear other people approaching you.

- Run/walk against traffic. If a car decides to pull over, you will see it slow down. If you are running/walking with traffic, you would never see it coming.

- Run in populated places or heavily run trails – make sure people see you

- Avoid areas that are perfect crime scenes

- When possible run with a buddy

- Learn self-defense

- If at a park get in the best position to gain awareness and be aware if anyone can come up from behind

INTERNET

- Check to make sure you are hitting secure links (https://) for banking/financial sites

- Keep your network hidden

- Have strong passwords for accounts and internet access

- Don't post details of travel until after. If you tell the world where you are, you are also letting them know where you are not.

- Don't blindly accept friends

- Keep your profiles private or secure

- Hackers are getting smart, don't play games or take surveys

- Don't click links in emails.....if it is a site that you visit, open another browser and type it in by hand.

- Have two accounts on your computer. 1 for administrator and 1 for the user. Only use the admin account when needed. Use the user account so that hackers can not get access to your system.

- Watch what you download. Verify it is what you want.

Notes

Notes

Notes

Notes

_____

_____

_____

_____

_____

_____

_____

_____

_____

_____

_____

CHAPTER 7
TECHNIQUES

SELF DEFENSE LAW

Before we get into physical techniques, we need to cover what self-defense is. Even though you are defending yourself, there is the line that can be crossed that goes from self-defense to attacker.

What is self-defense? (http://dictionary.law.com/ Default.aspx?selected=1909)

Self Defense Law - the use of reasonable force to protect oneself or members of the family from bodily harm from the attack of an aggressor, if the defender has reason to believe he/she/they is/are in danger. Self-defense is a common defense by a person accused of assault, battery or homicide. The force used in self-defense may be sufficient for protection from apparent harm (not just an empty verbal threat) or to halt any danger from attack, but cannot be an excuse to continue the attack or use excessive force.

Examples: an unarmed man punches Allen Alibi, who hits the attacker with a baseball bat. That is legitimate self-defense, but Alibi cannot chase after the attacker and shoot him or beat him senseless. If the attacker has a gun or a butcher knife and is verbally threatening, Alibi is probably warranted in shooting him. Appropriate self-defense is judged on all the circumstances. Reasonable force can also be used to protect property from theft or destruction. Self-defense cannot include killing or great bodily harm to defend property unless personal danger is also involved, as is the case in most burglaries, muggings or vandalism.

SURVIVAL MINDSET

Before we talk about your mindset, we need to cover fear. Many people become scared and freeze when they are faced with danger. They know that they are in danger, but they have not made up their minds to fight, or they are overwhelmed with what is happening and cannot mentally get a handle on what is going on. Maybe they have never been in this situation. Most people do not train to defend themselves, so they may not even know what to do. So what is fear?

Fear is an unpleasant emotion caused by the

belief that someone or something is dangerous, likely to cause pain or a threat. Fear is a vital response to physical and emotional danger—if we didn't feel it, we couldn't protect ourselves from legitimate threats

Fear is a great thing. It lets you know that you are in danger and is time to switch from victim to victor. You have to know that you are not going down without a fight. What helps here is to think of all the things that are important to you. Family, friends, kids, dogs, whatever it is, you make up your mind to fight, get to safety and be there for those who count on you. This is where your mindset has to switch to survival mode.

Let's say that you see a guy walking and get a feeling that something isn't right. You tell him to stop and to stay back and that you don't feel comfortable with him getting closer. He initially stops about 8-10 ft away, then suddenly comes in to get closer to you. It is at the very second your mind should switch and you either run away if possible or you strike first to get away.

The key to survival in any stressful situation is based on your ability to manage your thoughts, your anxiety, and your fears. In order to survive it is important that you take control of your mind. The natural reactions that your body will experience in a survival situation can help you do things you never thought possible.

It is important to remember that a violent situation can happen to anyone. Everyone will face something that they fear. Some people, think of fear as a weakness. As stated earlier fear lets you know that you are in danger and that something needs to be done. Fear is not the problem; it is what you do when you are forced to face that fear that is important.

TRAIN

To take the overwhelming feeling away from fearful thoughts it is important to train. This will allow you to be able to go to survival mode much easier. Train in real life situations as these will help you mentally prepare for something that could occur. There is no way to prepare for every situation, but you can develop a blueprint to build off of should something occur. Training will also help you to prevent freezing. You will overcome with fight or flight responses and training will help you to react to the situation rather think about what you have to do. Breathing is also essential to prevent the freeze.

What to do:

- Train and Develop Plan of Actions
- Observe and Orient yourself at all times (Situational Awareness)
- Based on the information that you are receiving from your environment make appropriate decisions
- After your decision(s) are made put them into action.
- Stay calm
- Stay in the present - Don't forecast the future. Opportunities will prevent themselves that you can take advantage of allowing you to get to safety if you are in the moment
- Believe in yourself
- Do whatever is needed to get to safety
- Never give up

Before we get into a few useful techniques, I wanted to say that there are three types of people who we could compare to wolves, sheep, and sheepdogs. Wolves are your predators/attackers; they are always on the hunt for the next victim. Your sheep are the people who may be unable to defend themselves or believe that there are not any bad people in the world. These could be kids, elderly, or perhaps individuals that grew up without experiencing violence. The sheepdogs are your protectors. They are the ones that know that the wolves exist and are willing to fight them if need be. These are people like police, military, security guards, and even parents, etc. If you have read this far, Congratulations, you are in the category of sheepdog as well.

I would say that 95% of the people walking around do not know how to fight technically. I'm not aware of many attackers that train in case they select a target that may put up a fight. The reason that a perpetrator has targeted you is that of real or perceived dominance. They are not expecting you to fight and statistically speaking you have a greater chance of getting away if your fight for your life. Perpetrators as a whole want an easy target, someone, that will not put up a fight, and they can dominate. These techniques are useful, easy to learn and you will be able to apply them immediately if you need to. Although I hope that you will never need to implement these techniques.

READY POSITION/DEFENSIVE STANCE

This is an excellent position to know. From this position, you have many options. You can block an attacker that is trying to overtake you; you can prevent strikes from your attacker, you can also deliver strikes to an attacker such as palm heels, front kicks, and knees.

This position is very similar to a boxing stance. Your feet should be shoulder width apart and at about 45-degree angle with your dominant leg in the rear. Your hands should be up and in front of your face with elbows down and close to your side. This position is important because if you are attacked your hands will already be in a position to block a punch to the face. You can also block wild punches that are intended to strike your head simply by bringing your forearms up to the side of your head.

PALM HEEL

In self-defense, the heel of your palm can be a more effective weapon than a closed fist, especially if you don't have experience throwing punches. If you are not trained to punch such as a boxer, then you risk injuring your hand or wrist when throwing your punches.

To execute a palm-heel strike, you will already be in you ready/defensive stance with your palm facing your attacker. Curl your fingers in to protect them leaving the heel of your palm exposed. Just like boxing throw your palm heel and make sure to get your hips into it by twisting them as you throw the strike. Strike the nose or chin with an upward motion, keeping your arm straight and using your body weight. Your lead hand is not as strong as the dominant hand. Throw a lead hand palm heel and immediately follow it up with the rear (power) strike.

FRONT KICK

The front kick can be delivered from the front, less powerful, or rear leg. Kicking with the rear leg is more common and more comfortable for most individuals. Kicking with the rear leg is a natural motion. It's easier for the kicker to shift their balance and put their weight and power behind the kick. To execute the kick, you will again start from your ready position with your open hands protecting your face. Bring your rear knee up and extend your leg out in front of you. With the kick, you can aim for the shin, knee, thigh, groin and abdomen areas. I would not go above that because if you miss you will be off balance or because you may not train often there is the chance that the attacker may see it coming and actually grab it.

KNEE

Your knees are a powerful weapon. The joint is large, hard and can cause a lot of pain. A knee strike to the groin is effective against both male and female attackers. This a close range attack. You can deliver this blow if your attacker is holding onto you, by only lifting your leg up with as much force as possible. If your attacker is pulling you toward them, use the momentum to land a painful knee strike straight into the groin.

To execute a basic knee strike, you will start from the ready/defense position. Reach up and clasp your fist tight. Doing this represents the fact that you are holding on to something of the attacker. This could be hair, ears, or clothes. Just make sure that you are holding onto them. Next, you will want to pull them down toward the ground with as much force as you can produce. While pulling them down, drive your knee into them. Depending on positioning, you can strike the groin, abdomen, leg or even head of your attacker.

TRAP AND ROLL

This move starts with the victim on her back and the attacker mounted on her chest.

1. Using both hands, the victim secures one of the

attacker's arms doing the best to pull the arm to her chest and places her foot with the same side foot of the attacker, keeping her elbows tucked in as much as possible.

2. The victim now lifts the attacker straight up with her hips and rolls on the same side as the arm and foot that are trapped, because the attacker has neither a hand nor a foot to stop him, he will topple over.

3. As the attacker begins to fall, the victim turns over going up to her knees, ending in the attacker's guard. From here the victim can proceed to punch the attacker in the ribs, abdomen, face, and then stand to stomp and kick the attacker before getting to safety.

This is an important technique as it can save you against an attacker that is punching your from the top or even applying a choke. The bridging (thrusting hips in high toward the sky) will throw the attacker off balance allowing the victim to effectively roll them over.

Other techniques that are easy to use are eye gouge, throat jabs, foot stomps, and biting. All of these are effective at defending yourself from attack.

Notes

Notes

Notes

Notes

CHAPTER 8
STORIES

A Seattle runner credits a self-defense class with helping her fight off an attack and attempted rape.

She stopped to use a public washroom at the park during the run when she was assaulted from behind by a man while she was washing her hands.

"He lunged at me and I immediately just started to go into fight mode."

He threw her on the ground and started punching her. She crawled into a stall, but he followed her and kept trying to turn her onto her stomach.

"All I kept screaming during the attack was, 'Not today, motherf***er.' I was screaming it like an animal. It was the most vicious savage part of my being. There was no way I was going to let this guy rape me," she said.

Three weeks beforehand, she'd participated in

a self-defense class through work, and remembered she should hit him with the side of her hand.

It took a long time for her to realize that she had been raped in a dorm in college.

"We were wrestling around," she said. "Things turned more sexual. I told him to stop. He thought I was joking. I froze."

Afterward, she brushed it off. But later, in her senior year, a flashback crystallized what had gone wrong, and she broke down sobbing.

Not long afterward, in the crowded basement of a fraternity house during a party, a drunk man stuck his hand up her skirt as she — sober — was walking past. She grabbed his hand, shoved it away and yelled at him to never touch her again. In that case, she filed a complaint with the college.

She later wrote an essay for the student newspaper in which she disclosed that her mother had been raped while she was a student at the same college in the 1980s.

"I am a legacy child in more ways than one," she wrote, "and I had inherited the rape culture on our campus that I'm sure she prayed would be gone by the time I got here."

Made in the
USA
Middletown, DE